OUT OF THE MUD
MAKE YOUR FUTURE YOUR PRESENT
BE GREAT NOW

Vernon A. Langley Jr.

Copyright © 2023 Vernon A. Langley Jr.

All rights reserved.

ISBN: 978-1-07602709-2

DEDICATION

To my late daughter, Ciara Janae Langley,
Vernon A. Langley Sr.

CONTENTS

1	**Graduation Day**	Pg 1
2	**The Night that Covered Me**	Pg 11
3	**My Unconquerable Soul**	Pg 20
4	**Failed Clutch of Circumstance**	Pg 32
5	**Bloody but Unbowed**	Pg 40
6	**Shall Find Me Unafraid**	Pg 51
7	**Master of My Fate**	Pg 60
8	**Captain of My Soul**	Pg 72

ACKNOWLEDGMENTS

Many thanks to my mother Madie C. Langley, my wife Antina R. Langley, my children Vernon A. Langley III, Ambria Langley and my late Uncle Joseph Wright.

To all my teachers and professors from Glen Oaks High School in Baton Rouge Louisiana and Southern University A & M College.

1 GRADUATION DAY

It seems like it was yesterday, I can remember waking up to the sound of the South Louisiana spring mating calls of a small bird on my window. The smell of dandelions and morning dew on St. Augustine grass, seeping through the rectangular window pane covered by the partial shade of a gray big window screen above my head.

As I lay in my twin bed, I arose to take a glimpse of the early morning sun reflecting off the window and burglar bars of my neighbor's house 10 feet away. Creating a prism of light seemingly created solely for the purpose of highlighting an eerie glow as if the light was coming in from a reflection of the Mississippi River herself. For a brief moment I was lost in the beauty of the Louisiana morning sunrise, cascading hues of brown, tan, rust and a shade of red.

Suddenly, I forgot what day it was as my eyes

became fixed on the brass coloring of a partially stable ceiling fan. It was graduation day, 1990 and, I had no reason to be excited. Knowing that today would be just a regular but not so regular day for me of course. As reality set in, I silently said to myself. I should be in school.

Knowing that my schedule says 11th grade it was my fourth year in high school. I would not have the luxury and excitement of participating in the ongoing events of today. Ashamed of the circumstances, I remained home to avoid the rhetorical questions if I went to school. Not questions of curiosity, just futile attempts to spark a reaction to justify a presumed pain I may be going through.

As I walked from my room, passing by music albums thumbtacked to my bedroom wall. A poster which stated "Do the Right Thing," alongside a picture of NWA and a Southern University Bayou Classic banner. I walked out of my bedroom passing through the dimly lit hallway into the main room of our home. Staring past brown paneling and volumes of the encyclopedia alongside multiple children's versions of the Bible. Both of which I had read dozens of times.

My mother, a very keen lady in her late fifties, dressed in her traditional nightgown was cooking the usual bacon, eggs and toast. Smoke filled the house from the perfectly burned bacon. I could smell the aroma of butter and everything that made breakfast my favorite meal of the day. Lost in the moment, I was interrupted by my mom saying good morning. Partially looking up and trying as always, my mother could see that I was not myself. She sighed, and uttered a low grunt and said graduation is today, huh?

I answered yes, and flopped onto the couch. Sinking into the warm cozy brown pillows, attempting to find peace and comfort from the thought process and energy of the day. I sat in silence, petting my little white foot terrier named Bootsie, staring at what appeared to be little white booties on his once black, but now gray feet. My attempt to find peace was futile.

My mother looked at me with a stern look on her face, one that would fit a Presidential State of the Union Address. My mother said son you're just as smart as any of those kids graduating today. You were reading the encyclopedia and the Bible by the age of two. You learned to spell your name as fast as you learned to say it. For some reason you have chosen not to be you. Not to be who you are capable of becoming.

You have your father's intelligence, and you look just like him. If you don't start living as who you are destined to be, you are going to stay believing you are who you are not. As I fell back onto the sofa, those words soaked into my inner spirit, as if I was the yellow sponge that she was cleaning with as she spoke to me. "Come here, sit down and listen."

As I entered our kitchen area taking a seat at our Maplewood and glass table. I observed my reflection on the glass cabinets, while preparing for a reality check as usual. "Vernon, you know who you are, you also know who you are capable of becoming. There is nothing small or mediocre about you." "You are a leader and one day you will be someone everyone will listen to."

"But Vernon, you are going to have to start becoming the man that your father knew you would become, the man that I know you are." Without saying a word, I stood up from the dining room table and walked outside once again taking in nature. Watching the sun rise through the five-story oak tree at the end of the block. I stood silently at the end of the driveway as tears rolled down my cheeks.

I thought to myself and asked why are you selling yourself short. There were no explanations, just tears.

> "There's no coming to consciousness without pain."
>
> - **Carl Gustav Jung**

Feeling lost, I returned outside, and I walked down the paved driveway slowly approaching the patio covered in that South Louisiana condensation. I walked a path that I've walked a million times before. This time it was different, this time my senses were heightened. This time I was awake.

I noticed a gray squirrel upside down staring up at me. I actually spoke to it. "Good morning little fella." I approached my backyard, taking a seat on the A/C unit. I shed a tear once more and watched as the fall leaves of brown and tan fell slowly to the ground. When I was young child, this was my thinking place. This is where I plotted, cried, thought and became inspired.

It's time to become who God made me to be.

As a child I was always reminded of my father's academic accomplishments. I was always told "your dad graduated from high school two years early, never made anything less than a B and joined the military at the age of 15. He was caught and re-enlisted at the age of 17. B's were never accepted in our home. C's were considered a failing grade as far as my father was concerned.

I dreamed daily of playing football with my neighborhood friends. In Louisiana, football is a way of life. It was normal to awake after a school nap to the smell of exhaust and the sound of blue jays and rusted pickup trucks stopping at various houses. Old dodge and ford horns blowing, while little football Warriors, Saints, Jaguars and various others would run out of their front doors, dragging shoulder pads covered with mesh practice jerseys and white football helmets in hand. "Come on boy, time for practice.

"Who Dat, Who Dat, Who Dat talking about

beating …" "We don't play sports in this house unless you get straight A's." I would cry, I wanted to play. I knew I was a smart kid, but I had not learned to overcome the elephant in the room.

My father was a great provider and a good dad. One of the few, black engineers working at the local nuclear plant in St. Francisville, Louisiana. My father was a middle-aged diabetic, battling with PTSD from serving in Korea, heart disease, racism and the fear of not living to see his two young boys grow into men.

While trying to make his 3rd attempt at marriage a successful one and hiding the pain of not seeing his two daughters, he self-medicated with alcohol. My father tended to become violent at times. Many nights my brother and I hid in the bedroom closet or under the bed, as my father would beat my mother. Boom, I would hear a thud, a touch of profanity and a scream. As fear overtook me, so did anger and rage.

A cocktail of emotions that hardened my soul and forged a version of me that had the ability to compartmentalize the moment. Which eventually evolved into the ability to compartmentalize weeks, then months, then years. The offspring of this cocktail was rage. A hidden rage that took every bit of my energy and focus to contain. There are many hills to overcome when a young man feels he can't protect his mother.

During these times of compartmentalization time stops and priorities sometimes take a back seat to natural instinct. Growing up in love and survival carries mixed messages that are not easily understood by young children. You just become numb and a shell of yourself. A shell, placed about you to protect you from the misunderstanding of love and hate, pain and confusion.

2 THE NIGHT THAT COVERED ME

Get up! I arose at a pace normally used to find change for the candy lady. I went into my bedroom. Locked the door, pulled out my senior memory book and wrote myself a letter. I identified my weakness.

It began on a summer day in Kansas, "everyone wake your tails up and get dressed." My mother was excited that my father was going to bar-b-que for my half-sisters whom he'd invited from New York. We had only seen them a few times during my ten years on this planet. I remembered my father crying himself to sleep many nights.

There was an obvious void that no one could fill. He wanted his daughters and his son who died from asthma years prior to me being born. My dad was a very stern, very direct man. Yet, as with many black men struggling to make their mark in a world, that repeatedly reminded them that they are a guest playing in this game called America. Struggling with alcoholism and regret, recovering from two heart attacks and two previously failed marriages.

It wasn't hard to notice that this fair skinned, 6-foot 1 statue of a man was watching his life play out like a movie. Still, he was laser focused on providing a better situation and improving the playing field for his two sons. When I was a child, I was always reminded of my father's academic accomplishments. I remember looking out of the screen door of our duplex on Cottonwood St. in Emporia Kansas.

Trees blowing to the backdrop of the William Allen White Mansion. My dad, in tears, on the grill and wearing his traditional white fruit of the loom t-shirt and khaki daddy shorts, striped sport socks and running shoes. I ask my mother, "what's wrong with daddy?" She stated he wanted to see his daughters. It was a normal day of bar-b-que and watching television. Walking outside, I could smell the aroma of summer.

The sky carried a dark blue hue, as a backdrop for the birds singing in harmony as if they had been waiting on summer forever. Black army ants paraded the sidewalk. Everything seemed to be in sync. For some strange reason I felt something was off, other than no one showing up for dinner. There was a sense of calm and peace as if I was watching life and life was staring back.

While sleeping in my room, I heard a thunderous sound as if a tree had fallen through the dark of night upon my neighbor's home. Suddenly there was a yell for help, as I launched from my bed and entered the front room. He lay there, as the room filled with medical personnel, the most powerful man on the planet. The other half of my soul. My father, dying from a massive heart attack.

Still wearing his tighty whites and a white V-neck T-Shirt. I began to compartmentalize the moment. I once heard that denial is the most predictable human response. With every bit of energy my ten-year-old legs could produce. I began sprinting barefoot through the freshly cut yard, then between the alleys of our duplexes.

I made a mad dash to the neighbor's home. Once there, I began to bang on the door "Help me please, my dad is dying." From there, silence! I have no recollection of anything from that point. Early the next morning my mother brought my brother and I into the den and told me and my brother that our father had passed away.

At that moment, half of who I was died. The next six years I simply existed. A month later, we moved back to Baton Rouge, Louisiana, I was numb, angry, bitter, and confused once again. My energy was negative, my spirit was numb and my heart was cold. Living through my perception of the world, my thoughts controlled me.

"What if I died? Who would be there for my family? Who's going to teach me how to be a man? Will my mother be able to love me and my brother as much as two parents? How are we going to be able to survive? Who is going to take care of us?

Due to my father's constant struggle with diabetes and heart disease. My mother and father had a contingency plan in place, in case anything ever happened to him. The plan was for us to move back to Baton Rouge. My father felt that Baton Rouge was still a budding town. Immune to all the big city problems that they were accustomed to, coming from New York. According to my fathers wishes we moved back to Louisiana.

At ten years old, I could not fully understand what was happening. Controlled by fear I fought, stole, lied, and cheated. I carried my pain on my shoulders. The pain of loss, the pain of confusion, the pain of the unknown. The following year I began to travel a very troublesome road.

During the next few weeks we moved back to Baton Rouge, with me entering the 5th grade. Luckily my dad had properly planned for the unthinkable, providing us with financial security through his life insurance policies. During this period, my mother showered us with toys, games and things that would keep us distracted from the pain of losing our father. Yet inside the darkness grew.

Louisiana has a magical way of allowing you to sink into the warmth of the misty sounds of mole crickets and the comforting backdrop of humidity. Yet a young mind has the ability to explore beyond the facade and clouded illusion of things being ok. After a year of denial, believing that my father had actually just gone away on business or to another job. I began to accept that things were going to be different forever. I began to accept that I would never wake up to the smell of fresh shaving cream and old spice coming from the hallway bathroom.

The background aroma of scrambled eggs, toast and bacon, the 4 A.M. sound of the car warming under the carport. A rhythmic melody that all young children call, daddy's leaving out for work. As I entered the sixth grade, things changed. School went from colorful classrooms to colorful gangs.

From the smell of crayons, to learning the smell of marijuana behind the building and which areas to avoid. The realization that the role of the Alpha Male was now mine. A strange fear that death would also call on me. Once again thrusting my family into despair and confusion.

Developing a fear of food poisoning, while my young mind tried to wrap itself around the concept of death and living a full life. Anger became my coping mechanism. Anger for my teachers, mom, peers, just anyone in general. Today it would be called Oppositional Defiant Disorder. I called it "Just pissed the hell off." During this period of my life roughly 6th - 8th grade, the story stayed the same.

I refused to cooperate in school in any shape, form or fashion. Slowly falling behind academically, yet still having enough prior knowledge to sufficiently make it to the next grade level. After three years of not applying myself, I entered the 9th grade at Glen Oaks High School in Baton Rouge, Louisiana.

Things at this point just became a blur. First day of school, 13 years old, the smell of fresh Calvin Klein jeans starched and creased. Brand new "Catch the Wave" Coca-Cola shirt and Nike Air Force Ones with a hint of Aramis cologne. We lived about 1300 meters from the school, with a mile consisting of 1600 meters, the school system did not provide bus transportation.

"Hey little dude, hop in." "Clink, Clink, the sound of a loose muffler and suspension. The smell of carbon dioxide and the laughter of 10 teenage boys piling into a station wagon driven by one of the neighborhood fellas. This was our school bus, the "Hood Mobile." "The Ghost."

During these times my mind shifted to masking the pain of not having what I considered half of my identity. I would dream that he would come home from work. Then awake to find that it was all a dream. Carrying that anger to school the next day became my burden, my truth, and my suffering.

3 MY UNCONQUERABLE SOUL

> "The root cause of our suffering is our own thinking."
>
> - **Joseph Nguyen**

"Oh Shit", as I walked down the hall, face looking down at my class schedule. "F" building, the smell of old Formica and ceiling tiles. The whiff of some experiment Mrs. Fault was conjuring up for the first day of school, to spark the students interest placed in her Chemistry class. I peeped in, to see bunsen burners going.

With a heightened sense of interest and awareness, I hear "Oh Shit!" "I got to teach your black ass." "I can't stand your little badass." "Get your head out of Mrs. Fault's Class. That isn't for you." Hurt and confused at what I was told, I immediately felt a cold pain run down the center of my chest as if the hurt had become liquified and was pouring into my Aorta.

Come on Mrs. Beemer, I replied. You know you love me. This somewhat softened the blow that made me feel as if I was less than anything worth becoming. Had I really painted an image of myself that was repulsive to my teachers? As I sat and pondered that thought as many young men do as members or victims of the American educational system.

What did I do so obnoxious as a young man that would make my teachers believe that growth was not possible? Had I changed for the better? I don't know? What I do know is this isn't my true self. This isn't who I wanted to be. As a young man, especially as a young black man. My voice wasn't always vocal.

Do my teachers see the pain in my eyes? Do they feel the sense of despair in the heart of a young man seeking his position in this world; without the guidance and security of a black male role model in the home. Throughout the day I carried the burden of that thought process.

"Good afternoon, students, faculty and staff." As the principal began the afternoon announcements. He was interrupted by the school bell. Thank God, day over. The next day as I awoke to the bright rays of sunlight, creating those morning shadows through my mini blinds, that created a perfect backdrop for the consistent concert of sounds created by those Louisiana mole crickets. I got out of bed making a wobbly morning stroll past the mahogany coffee table that my mom kept all the mail on.

I saw the letters ACT on an envelope resting on the table. Wanting to reach for it, I leaned in, anxiety began to creep in. The overwhelming fear that my teachers had a valid point as to what type of person I was, overtook my movement. I remained frozen. Just as if, I was standing in a solid lake of regret.

Being a strong student prior to my father's death. The next few years I remained unmotivated, doubted, and ignored. I believed that the ACT would provide proof that I intellectually was capable of high achievement. Proof that I will still be a factor in this game called life.

Knowing that on the day of the ACT, I slept 1 hour and 10 minutes of the 2-hour test, after going to the Club Dreams the night before. Finally, I overcame my fear, I reached for the envelope and opened it. My score falsely confirmed to me what Mrs. Beemer made me feel. Dam, I failed to prove my worth.

After a few weeks had passed, and the pain subsided. I was dressed in Girbauds and a Polo top listening to Biz Markie ``Vapors'' walking in the Cortana Mall. During this day, I stopped at the Naval recruiter and stated I'm a hard worker and I need your hardest training regimen, "Seal Training." The recruiter informed me that I needed to focus on school first. The next day at school, I walked into the gym for my Physical Education class, excited, focused and strangely happy that I scored 14 sleeping on the ACT.

I realized "I am worthy," I didn't think I could have scored that awake. Had I allowed myself to sink that fast in three 3 years? As class ended, I walked with a sense of purpose up the hill to the basketball gym. Excited, motivated, encouraged and enthusiastic about getting an encouraging response from one of the few teachers that I imagined believed in me.

I waited outside the locker room doors waiting to give my physical education coach the news. I hadn't pissed him off too much this year. Maybe he will be proud to hear that I'm going to go for a high score. Maybe he will uplift my spirit. Coach looked at me and said, with a stern face.

Vernon, go to the military. You are not college material.

Those words cut like a razor-sharp knife. Immediately and painfully crushed, "I awoke, at last." Never again will I allow myself to be doubted, to be told that I'm inadequate, game on, I thought!

"Once the game is over, the King and the pawn go back in the same box."

– Italian Proverb

I was once told that life is undefeated, it kills everyone. The day I heard that, I decided that we are all going to die participating in the game, then why not enjoy the fight. We have one chance to be the best version of ourselves. I truly believe that life brings a fair game to us. A game that is tailored to respond to our individual talents and abilities.

We are all told that life doesn't give us anything that we can't handle. I feel this way because we are equally matched by life. Here's the kicker, life doesn't adjust to us not being the best version of us. We must rise to the occasion to persevere. I truly believed that once presented with a challenge we all have the innate ability to meet that challenge head on.

Walking along Glen Oaks Drive, making my way back to that old forest heights subdivision "The Flip". I began to once again take in life. I began to absorb that sweet smell of pine as I neared Silverleaf Drive. That smell of humidity soothed my soul, as I allowed the birds to sing into my spirit. I began to see myself once again as I had always done growing up.

I began to see life as an opportunity, as a canvas in which to paint my story of success. Hello mama, as I walked in the door. It was all about corn flakes and textbooks. Time to play catch up in this race. I had a hurdle or two.

Time to dig in and get back into this race. After successfully bringing my grades up in school and starting to dream again. For the first time since my father's death. I began to really take school seriously. Celebrating at the pep rally with what I thought was my graduating class.

I got a call to come to guidance and meet with Mrs. E. Our senior guidance counselor. Mr. Langley you may go to the office, stated Mrs. West. Happy that I get to take a brief walk and get out of class. I was also excited to tell Mrs. E. of my new perspective on life.

I walked to the front office, totally oblivious to what was about to transpire. Entering the front glass doors, I spoke with the school secretary. Mrs. E said "sit down Mr. Langley," yes ma'am. "Mr. Langley, I'm sorry to inform you that you will not graduate again this year."

"What are you talking about Mrs. E." I have good grades now." "Yes, Mr. Langley, but you have two years of classes that you are making up." "Hell no, I replied." I grabbed My books and threw them on the floor and said. I'm out."

"I'm not going to come back with my little brother. I stormed out of the front office. Faced by the humid and steamy air of Baton Rouge, Louisiana. I walked one mile through acorn covered sidewalks and 98-degree weather.

As I approached my house. I could see my mom in the kitchen window. I could feel that she knew. As I entered, my mom stated "so you quit huh." Well, time to go get a job. Can't live here as a grown man and not be in school. I got back in my car and began the task of looking for a job while I figured out my next move.

Starting with McDonald's, I acquired a few jobs and became the typical high school dropout. Trying to earn a living in America with no skills, no education and no true concept of what the future held.

My career as a dropout began two weeks later

as a night porter at McDonalds. Honest money, but a bit demeaning. My job was to arrive at McDonald's 10 pm. at night. During this time, I began changing the fry vats and making trash runs. Afterwards the lobby would close and the management would lock the doors and I would begin cleaning the restrooms, trash bins and under the tables.

I had three hours to clean the store top to bottom while locked in the store without any keys. When the employees arrived at 4:00am. I made the final trash runs while battling the raccoons for room around the trash bins.

I noticed this was particularly amusing to the morning crew, as the raccoons, which looked to be the size of a T.rex, chased me across the parking lot as if it was an early morning track meet. The job was a humbling experience.

I would ask myself, am I more than amusement for a morning breakfast crew? One of the greatest artists in history once said. "I'm looking at the man in the mirror." We sometimes have to stop and ask ourselves. Are we living our best life? Are we built for better highways than the ones we are currently traveling? Life simply responds. The Bible states that greater is in him than he that is in the world.

With that being said, "The greatest version of you lie within." Would you not expect a snake to bite you? Would you not expect a dog to chase you if you ran? A lion raised in a cage still needs the cage locked because he instinctively knows there is more. These are qualities you have that exist within.

Your true nature must be dug from under the years of people attempting to download a program of you that will not bring them any discomfort. A program they can understand. The true and best version of you is not meant to be understood by anyone but you. The best version of you is greater than anyone can help you become. It can only be brought out by you.

Test life, go for it all. Make life respond, expect failure, hurt, grief, and pain. Also expect growth, power and perseverance. Wake up anew every day.

4 FAILED CLUTCH OF CIRCUMSTANCE

With all teenage boys approaching manhood. I began to feel what I thought was maturity running through my veins, as the old folks would say. I began to smell myself. After a long night of coffee, developing a runny nose from falling asleep while sitting in my Mazda RX-7 with the AC on high.

I made a futile attempt to find comfort, while pulling a security detail in a dark humid 98-degree parking lots in mid-city. This was following a long day, fighting raccoons and rats while attempting to make trash runs and cleaning fry vats. I decided to move about with a winning attitude. I awoke to Vernon, you better clean that damn bedroom, I closed my door and blasted my two 15-inch sub-woofers in an attempt to act like I was grown and moving at my own groove.

Boom, there was a loud crack as my mom, dressed in her nightgown and slippers politely kicked open my door and said. "Get this room cleaned before I call your Uncle. By way of Norfolk, Virginia, my only uncle, "Uncle Duddy". A local Automotive Instructor at the technical college. A strong-willed, strong-minded hardworking man.

Uncle Duddy moved to Louisiana 12 years prior and built a wonderful life for himself, at the age of 48. My uncle spent countless hours attempting to help my mom raise two little knucklehead boys. Yet, this time one of us, myself, decided today he's a man. "Call that dude, I am a grown man." Instead of my mom going upside my head. She had a look of fear that I have never seen before. "Leave the house Vernon. He's on his way."

That look was enough. At that moment I saw Uncle Duddy, pistol in hand, walking up the driveway. I hopped out of the back window and ran to my homeboy's house. I need to lie low for a snap. After a few hours of video games and a few snacks. I went back home, and entered the house back through my bedroom window not seeing his car in the yard. I figured the coast was clear. "Come here," from behind the dining room. Uncle Duddy appeared faster than I could react and make a move for the window. I swung, he ducked, bobbed and that's about all I remember, until I came to, upside down against the wall. Realizing quickly that I wasn't grown yet. After a discussion about respect and manhood. My uncle said I love you son, and left. Next morning, time to reflect. For some strange reason. I had convinced myself that I had become a man.

    Dam, I thought, there's a whole different level to that game. Hot air, steamy concrete, the buttery pungent smell of wild flowers and humidity mixed with the warm smell of wild magnolias. The sound of 18-wheeler rigs shifting gears, Blue Jays and a faint smell of natural gas as it creeps along the Old

Mississippi River and through South Baton Rouge. The calming effect of a slight splash here and there. "The Lakes at LSU."

My place, my peace. I exited the Interstate near the famed I-10 historic McKinley High School's one lane situation prior to the 10/12 split. I began to run, taking in the other side of life. I thought about how I grew up only 6 miles away. It was right here I had never really looked at the lake before. I ran, passing by southern charm, beautiful landscapes, and a million-dollar fraternity houses. I questioned my position in the game. Is there another board or am I on the wrong side of the board?

"You got to get up, get out and get something. Don't let the days of your life pass by. You got to get up, get out and get something. Don't spend all your time trying to get high." "I don't recall ever graduating at all." A voice played across the radio as if I was speaking to myself. I pulled over. "Sometimes I feel I'm just a disappointment to y'all." It was a young rap group on the radio called Outkast. "I agree, I got to be the man I was supposed to be." Wow, I stopped. I asked myself am I the man I'm supposed to be.

"To get what you love, you have to be patient with what you hate"

-Author Unknown

I gassed up an old soiled pressure washer. Standing on ten toes aching from the bitter humid 21-degree air freezing my feet as if they were a pack of cold franks wrapped in a pair of boat shoes. I stood frustrated and cold in preparation to remove as much oil from the second window drive through at Mickey D's. I once again found myself questioning every move I've made over the past 5 years. "Mr. Langley, we need you inside." I entered I noticed the strange distant look of my co-workers.

A look of hope that my answer to the question would relieve the pressure of what task was on the menu. After making my way across the lobby, I opened the door to the women's bathroom. After propping it open, using a garbage can from the bin. I was hit with a pungent odor, seemingly from the pits of hell. "Mr. Langley, you're on deck.

It's your turn to get the bathrooms." Hell no, I replied. Another pivotal moment was in the making. Looking my manager in the eye, why do you suppose it's my turn? His stated, "because you're the only one here not in school. Bye, I quit.

That was it, the end of my fast food career. I would not be denied. The next morning, I drove back to my old high school. Entering the office lobby surrounded by multiple district championships won by our long-time basketball coach. I walked through the double doors.

I remember telling myself to be humble and firm. "Good morning Mr. Langley. What do you need." "I need to graduate. Can I speak with guidance?" "Come on back." Good afternoon Mrs. E. I came in to find out what I need to do to graduate. Mrs. E said in a calm, nice relaxed tone as if she was my grandmother about to ask if I wanted that last slice of apple pie. "You need to be willing to make sacrifices, baby.

"Great success requires greater sacrifice."

- **Sachin Prabhu**

Mrs. E handed me the info for a summer school session in town. Embarrassed of my situation and not wanting everyone in the world that two years after my graduating class had marched. That I was still without my high school diploma. "Sorry, Mrs. E. I'm not that humble yet. Is there a summer school offered in a nearby town? She said yes.

Across the river in Port Allen. I headed west. Driving across what we call the old Mississippi Bridge." Passing by the rusted iron. I rolled down the window to smell the pungent odor of chemicals and humidity rising above the deepest part of the Mississippi River quietly yet powerfully making that beautiful turn, overlooking the Bluff of Southern University. "I will be there soon."

5 BLOODY BUT UNBOWED

"When you see a man skilled in his work, he can walk amongst Kings."

-Proverbs 22:29

The next morning, I once again awoke to the smells of mom's deep-fried bacon sizzling amongst the warm smell of eggs and buttery toast. Excitingly motivated to make my way past the sun lit curtains and orange glow of the morning sun rising through the large live oak tree standing powerfully outside our patio window. "Guess what?" I'm going to college in the fall. Hoping to get a celebrated response.

I was met with a stare of doubt. "Boy you just want to go chase those girls." If you're going to go to school you have to be serious about what you are trying to do. After that, High school was immediately erased from my consciousness. I compartmentalized that entire segment of my life. I killed him.

The version of me that could no longer exist if I'm going to become the man I'm supposed to be. I adopted a philosophy that I follow to this very day. The goal is to put my head on a pillow every night, then awake the next day a better man than the one who removed it from the pillow this morning. I believe that life will always be challenging and that it will always meet us where we are.

We have two options. Meet that challenge as the same individual as we were the day before or meet it as a new man. Just a little bit or maybe a lot better due to experience.

"You have to die a few times before you can really live."

Bukowski

I began feeding my subconscious at a level unprecedented by anything I had ever done before. I began to take in life. Anything that pointed toward success I began to digest. I began to read everything I could find on the subject of success. I wanted to re-write my entire programming.

I was on a mission to create a new consciousness. During my transformation I trained my mind, body and soul. Everyday became a challenge. At night as a security guard, I would work the dog shifts from 10pm-5am sitting in my car walking around cold or hot humid empty parking lots making rounds. It wasn't long before I learned that there was peace in the night.

A sense of calm that exists nourishing our soul and allows us to escape life, light and time. It allows us to move beyond our troubles, into a place where our true self reigns supreme. Sometimes I ran during my security rounds, often ten flights of stairs of humid filled, puddle soak parking lots. It didn't matter. Whatever I could use to be better myself mentally, spiritually and physically.

Success comes to the man who has no off switch, toward his personal goal towards perfection.

I began to work in silence, on becoming the ultimate version of me. Anything that I found myself to be talented at, I worked tirelessly at mastering that skill. As I attempted to remain asleep, trying to ignore the loud buzzing of that dark brown monster with orange digital eyes rested on my nightstand. I awoke, kicking back the twin sheets and reaching over to hit the snooze button. I would place my feet on the tile popping up and throwing on a pair of sweatpants and T shirt.

Rushing in and out of the bathroom as if the house was on fire. I jumped in my 1982 Mazda RX-7 and made the 20-minute trip across what us Baton Rouge folk called the old Mississippi Bridge to Port Allen Louisiana. Going over to Port Allen Junior High School and sitting in an 85-degree classroom next to Mississippi levee where I took Algebra II and English III. After a summer of mentally and physically focusing on me. Also, after completing a few college prep courses in summer school that would guarantee my entrance into college.

I applied to Southern University. "Wake up Vernon, wake up Vernon you have mail." As always, my mother was dressed in her traditional nightgown. A blurry vision of my mother stood in my doorway, as I wiped the cold and sweat brought on by the July heat from my eyes. "Open it, Open it."

I reached for the envelope, scared but confident, happy but extremely nervous. "Mr.

Langley, we are pleased to inform you of your admission into Southern University of Baton Rouge Louisiana for the fall 92' semester." Excited, Running, dancing and celebrating the achievement of my first goal. I paused and reminded myself, there is much work to be done. Time to prove all those people who thought that I would never make anything of myself wrong.

"What are you doing up here?" My first challenge, as I walked across the humid campus feeling a sense of fear. Seeing one of my friends' moms from the block. I felt a buildup of excitement come over me. Assuming that I was about to be praised for my accomplishment she actually blurted from her vehicle.

What are you doing here? Prior to that moment I was actually excited about the opportunity to tell her that I'm going to college. Shot down like a duck over a lake. My spirit was crushed. That statement ignited my fire.

GAME ON! "Hats off in the building." "Have your own pencil ready." "Pull those pants up". The opportunity to absorb and grow was everywhere. What better examples of black excellence could I ask for.

"Know thyself, know thy enemy. A thousand battles, a thousand victories. "-Sun TZU

The maxim, or aphorism "know thyself" is one of the strongest maxims ever stated. It is simply called self-awareness. A must in any battle, competition, or challenge. I believe that winning and losing in life, in your marriage, family and on your job is largely influenced by understanding where you exist, where you stand in relation to your dreams, your goals, your associates and even your competitors.

Some would ask who are my competitors? First, I would say myself. The next answer is, anyone that's aiming at similar goals and has the ability to affect the outcome of your race. Your race, (pause) most of us do not know that we are in a race. Unfortunately, some of us never will until it is too late. Lane 5 the undefeated champion from your local town (you).

As a youth I ran an event called the 400mH. One complete lap around the Track. It is the longest sprint and arguably the most painful event in the sport. It is an event that requires not only hard work, but you must be blessed with a certain amount of talent (speed).

There is another distinctive characteristic. This race has the most notable stagger of all the events run on the track. There is 50.23 meters between lane 1 and lane 9. That's 6.28m between each lane. This is due to the outside lane having to naturally run 50.23 meters further. So as the runners step on to the track and they are placed in their lanes one would ask.

Who gets to run the shortest race? 90% of the time they will say lane 9. That is because the individual appears to have a head start. When I ask who has the greatest disadvantage most say lane 1 because he starts behind everyone. Well, in a track meet, lanes are assigned or seeded by times.

The competitors with the best time will be assigned the lanes closest to the middle. "the best lanes" why? They Earned it. As a result, they will have a greater opportunity to feel where they stand in relation to the other runners during the race. They have a better view of the field. In the 400m the stagger doesn't come true until the 300m mark or ¾ the distance of the race.

Understanding this, the runner will know that if a person pulls up beside you on your inside and stays side by side with you. They will be 6.28 meters ahead of you when you come out of the second curve. If there are two lanes to your inside they will be 14.56 meters ahead. Well life works similar to the 400m dash. Some individuals must begin their race in what may appear to be dire circumstances.

They are unaware that the key to true success in becoming the best version of themselves is to exist at your potential. Run your best race, focus on winning your lane. Some individuals are blessed to have the resources available to them to gauge where they exist in the race. These resources may be highly educated parents, great relationships, friendships or just a keen awareness of self. Others may be given what appears to be a head start.

Yet, making them aware of the grind and potential that also exist with the race. Regardless of the circumstances in life or in track and field, run your race. You will find yourself in it for the win. You will find your dreams and aspirations chasing you. Because you have reached your ultimate existence, allowing life to react to the powerful energy you emit as you master and reach your ultimate existence.

6 SHALL FIND ME UNAFRAID

One day a young man was sitting on the beach against a rock crying. A stranger walked up and asked the young man if everything was ok? The young man sadly looked up and said not really. The stranger stated, may I ask why? Well since you asked, said the young man.

I'm realizing that life is hard, and I would like to be a successful person one day. Everything I do, I fail at. I'm afraid that my dream may never come true. The stranger asked what are your dreams? No one had ever really asked the young man what his dreams were before.

This question made him take a second look at the person to whom he was speaking with. The stranger was a man not much taller than himself, approximately 20 years his senior. Wearing a pair of hospital scrubs and a stethoscope, He had a familiar look in his eye that the young man couldn't place. The young man stood up and said I want to be like you. Apparently, you are a doctor.

The stranger stated no, I am a man first. I was once a young man, as you are today. I remember feeling that I could never accomplish my dreams of becoming a top surgeon in the medical field. Feeling that it was going to take too long, was going to be too hard, that I would mess it up along the way, there are people smarter than I.

The young man asked, then how did you do it? Well young man, I made it, my now. I became a doctor that day 20 years ago. I got out of my way and became my future self. I began to think like a doctor, walk like a doctor, talk like a doctor, prepare like a doctor, and preserved as a doctor. Today son, I am here to uplift you as the doctor you already are.

Suddenly, the wind blew and a chill grew in the air, and there was a tap on the young man's shoulders. Excuse me sir, stated another stranger, wake up it's going to get pretty chilly out here soon. The young man rose up abruptly, looked around. To his left, then to his right, the man in the scrubs was nowhere in sight. He realized at that moment he had met his future self that night!

Here is where you will find yourself unafraid. Silently, I approached my daily goals as if they were gems in a riverbed. I was once told that he who looks outside dreams, He who looks inside awakens." Without fail, fear, insecurity or regret. I began my grind.

Never thinking of or allowing myself to fear failure. I remember sitting on the back of my truck fishing at my favorite watering hole watching how nature gathered together to dance to a subtle but great dance of unity. A thought came to mind. As I cast my recreational pole into the lake taking in the balance of nature and allowing myself to really dream for the first time in years. I thought about how life works.

I thought I'd take in a lesson from the most unlikely of beings. The fish, yes, the fish. When we fish we consider it a sport, yet the fish are unwilling participants as they believe they are participating in a natural game of survival of the fittest. Yet there is a lesson to be learned. The fish are unknowingly aware of the impending danger of man. This is because the fish are engaged and found unafraid.

It fears not, because it is focused on a goal. Taking in that observation, I tracked along. My goal was to return to my former high school in my community and uplift someone, anyone facing doubt, anger, pain, isolation, fear, lack of understanding. So, from there I worked.

Life is about challenges, this is what makes us human. Without challenge how do we define life, how do we define greatness, how do we define success. One must overcome something. (A challenge) in order to be declared the victor, the champion or even the accomplished. I was once told that the way someone feels can be determined by the way one acts. (Thanks mom).

If you desire to be great. Be Great! Don't wait for life to come along singing and ringing bells as if you are in the school yard of failure or anxiety and the success bell rings and suddenly you're great. Life and this universe are simply energy and action. Life will respond to you or you're going to be forced to respond to it. The choice is yours.

Have you ever awakened from a nightmare and your entire day felt dark? I begin to climb out of the dark by waking up daily and bringing light to my dreams. "You do not sing because you're happy, you may be happy because you sing." The author Anna Right once wrote. "Let us assume nothing, and we shall not be mortified." "I am what I pretend to be. About me there is no make believe."

Be the artist that creates you! You are your own canvas. What if God made you into an artist, and commissioned you to create the ultimate portrait of life. The canvas, you, the theme of success, the mechanism, your spirit. Where do you begin? Where do you derive your inspiration? Do you look within? Do you look for an outside opinion about yourself?

Too many times in life. We focus and give too much energy to what we believe the world thinks of us. We allow that energy a place on our canvas. Well I've got news for you. This is a real scenario.

God has given you that canvas, it is your destiny, your obligation to all of his glory to embrace your spirit and go to work. It is your responsibility to be great, your responsibility to grow, and your responsibility to sit in the front of that class.

Be the first player on the practice field. Last man leaving the weight room. First man at work. Last man to leave. It is your responsibility to be innovative. Present that new idea, take that challenge.

Fight that sleep and study until you know it. It was mid-afternoon, as I arrived home from work. After working the entire night cleaning fry vats, running trash, and washing windows. I arrived at home to find my dog lying in the middle of the living room floor. Vernon, take that dog to the Vet. Clinic.

Not wanting to be bothered I loaded up my 90 lb. German Shepherd Rottweiler mixed and headed out. Once arriving, turning off Plank Road and onto those white and tan colored gravel rocks that would be the stepping stones that would point me in the direction of working with great men and women of character and dedication.

Good afternoon, welcome to Plank Road Veterinary Clinic. Entering the room from a small door located behind the counter was a man of prestige. "What do you need, young man." I responded, my dog is acting strange and my mom told me to bring him here. "Well, you brought him to the right place for that." 'We will get you into a room." as I stood silently amazed.

I had never seen a black Veterinarian before. Watching him work, I had to ask. Excuse me Doc, what would I have to do to become a Veterinarian? Looking at me through brown rimmed glasses. He said, be the best version of yourself, and you can be anything you want to. For the first time in years, someone spoke life into me. Someone actually looked and didn't see a janitor, a class clown, a failure, a dropout.

After the visit, I said thank you sir. His reply, "for what son?" I responded, for seeing me as something more. I told Dr. Raby I dropped out of high school and I don't think the world or anyone in it cares. He stated, "Is not their responsibility to care. It's yours."

Once in the car, I cried, I cried for every moment that I let myself down. I cried, for every time I argued with my mother when she told me that I was failing myself and allowing people to outperform me in life. For everything I wanted to be and everything I knew I could become. I cried, and began to act.

After dropping off my dog at home, I drove over to my girlfriend's house. There was one thing I listened to from Uncle Duddy. A strong man needs a strong woman in his corner. A strong woman is your backbone when you are tired. She becomes your energy when you run low. Last, a strong woman will merge her spirit with yours when you are at your lowest.

So, I went to see my off and on girlfriend from 11th grade throughout high school and after dropping out. There was only one person that spoke life into me when I was at my lowest cleaning toilets. I said I'm going to college and major in Animal Science Pre-Vet. Her response, "let's do it.

7 MASTER OF MY FATE

Someone once asked me, do you always insist on taking the hard road? I replied, "Why do you assume I see two roads?"

Committed are those who choose to be great. When everyone simply asks why. They just go to work. Put their hands in the dirt. Then hustle without a reply. There are those that claim their excuses are valid. There are those that assume they are lost. There are those that look for the path that's least traveled. Uncharted as the sailor replied. Because there lies the gold. The success of the soul who, chooses to not be denied.

When it's all said and done, we choose to have fun. We dance to the tune of success. It won't matter the cost. For it was not a loss. It was our fears we had to suppress. Then we dug in the dirt and we put in that work. When we looked up, there was nothing left. What we conquered was great. Yet, we made no mistake, because they all had given their last breath.

"As a man thinketh, so he is, and as he continues to think, so he remains."

- **James Allen**
-

Many times, I would be asked about my process. How did you go from dropout to college graduate? Being able to answer that question. I would think for a second and reflect on the current thought process. Look into the eyes of the individual asking in hopes of providing a rational explanation.

When in reality, I never really thought of the process as a problem. The process is always and will always remain a process. August Fall 1992 as I approached what is referred to as the hump. A bridge in the Scotlandville area of Baton Rouge, Louisiana. As a young boy, I crossed this bridge many times as a youth track & field athlete.

As I rolled down the windows on my ride removing the top from the RX-7. I began to take in the familiar aroma of the Mississippi River located just under a mile from Scenic Highway. and Scotland Avenue. The familiar sound of a train as it passes through the Ville and onto the refinery's located along the river. The early morning sun shining through the back-window casting Earth's shadow atop A.W. Mumford Stadium. Rims shining, cars waxed, and speakers booming.

I approached what we refer to as the yard and made my typical youthful round, scoping out what I felt the yard had to offer. I found a parking space. As I turned off the vehicle, I asked myself. Am I really here? Walking along a path I would walk thousands of times more.

I passed under the two large oak trees along

the north end zone and onward to what would be the next six part time and full-time years of college. I didn't dive into it without caution. I can recall my first registration on the yard. As any Jaguar will tell you, it will be your first test of faith. Be on time, stand in line. Don't forget anything in the car, not even your soul. As I entered what is known as the SU men's gym still taken by the opportunity to attend college I met with my advisor.

Due to my low ACT scores, I had to take remedial classes. I decided, I would go to school part time. I approached a small desk located on the gymnasium floor surrounded by 400 anxious students, praying to get the registration complete in just one day. Some had done this dance many times. Others had no idea that they will spend the next four days trained by frustration and hardened by impatience.

Excuse me Miss. How many classes do you have to take to be considered full time? Having $450 in my wallet and no knowledge about school cost, financial aid, grant opportunities, or a single person on the planet who supported me going to college. I was in for a rude awakening. "Sir, twelve hours is roughly one thousand dollars." Well, how many classes can I take for $450?"

The clerk looked me in the eyes and asked me the question I most feared, why are you even here? My reply, I want to get into school. "Maybe you should wait a semester and save some money." I'm a janitor at McDonalds. I sit in empty parking lots in a security uniform watching life pass me by as consistently as the stars in the sky.

I can't go another day with that being my identity. If I only have the money for one class, that is what I will do. I will just have to take one class. Feeling as if I was on trial, I was reminded of the promises that I made to myself. Ma'am I will take one class a semester if that's what I have to do.

I can no longer "clean up shit." She laughed, then stated I understand. I was once told that when a ship is at sea facing rough waters it must keep its bow pointing into the waves to plow through them safely, since a massive wave striking the ship's side could roll the vessel over and sink it. If there is one thing that I have learned about life is that adversity will find you. Some days life can be calm and welcoming seas.

These days will come and go. These are the days we wish for. Finances on point, friendships balanced, and feeling as healthy as a bull. Other days, life can be rough and treacherous. Those days seem as if everything we touch will fail.

There will come a day that life will continue to pound on us as if we are ships at sea. During these times we must prepare. We must be ready to push forward and plow through the waves. We must create our own energy. By doing this, I promise your life will get out of your way just as the waves in the ocean do.

My plan was to add a class each semester until I could afford to go to school full time. Without any guidance from anyone, I was not informed of many payment options, such as financial aid until my 4th semester of college. I just knew that failure was not an option. I just reminded myself that there are two types of people in this world. Finishers and quitters.

I soon came to realize that circumstances are never a factor. Finishers will always find a reason to finish and quitters will always find a reason to quit. Every day one must find a reason to finish. Life will always change and so we must also adapt and adjust to that chance. Our reasons for beginning our journey must also change.

That reason must be allowed to grow and evolve, so that It will match what life has in store. Remember Einstein showed us that Matter and Energy are the same thing. One must create balance in their life during times of trouble by simply responding to negative energy with equal and opposite positive energy. I was once told that the problem is never the problem. The problem is a problem when we have a negative response to the problem.

We must enthusiastically embrace our process. We can harness our greatest abilities, when there is no energy of doubt within. During these times of total belief or (faith) we have the ability to tap into what we were ultimately designed to be. The individual that was so great as a single cell that we outperformed millions and entered into this world.

There are always stories of humans carrying out miraculous feats and achievements. When the reason for which to accomplish the feat is great enough to push through to a person's subconscious. Making doubt or fear unrecognizable. At times when this happens, we accomplish great feats unrecognizable in our current conscious state.

There was once a man who planted a seed in the most fertile soil on his land. As the seedling became a beautiful tree it produced the tastiest fruit for years. One day the man was told that since the tree was established he could remove it from its present spot and place it in a less fertile soil bed. Over time, the tree no longer produced the same quality of fruit it once did.

Frustrated, the man pulled the tree up and replanted it back in the soil from which it came. The fruit of our being are the thoughts that guide our daily decisions most of the day. They become our subconscious. In order to overcome the adversity that awaits us in our path to our goals and dreams. We must keep ourselves planted in the proper soil.

Soil that nourishes our subconscious. When we plant ourselves in the wrong soil or in an environment that doesn't properly nourish our subconscious thoughts. We allow the negative energy and events to rewrite our subconscious. Causing us to produce poor fruit (negative thoughts that do not support dreams and goals).

Throughout college I never thought about failure or high school. I was engaged in living life to the fullest. As I went to my first class, I remember fear setting in. Do I belong here? Did I pay my dues by doing my school work in High School to the fullest?

Knowing that there was no one in the world that believed in me. Not many individuals, speaking life into me. It was going to be totally up to me. I remember walking under the Live Oak tree along the sidewalk and up the stairs my first day in fisher hall. The smell of old brick, mildew and Formica coming from the bathrooms as one entered the foyer.

The sound of vending machines and students mumbling and conversing. As we all made our way to class as Dean St. Amant reminded us to take off our hats in the building. Class was packed, I wasn't the only one needing remedial reading. I picked up my syllabus, although it was my first time hearing the word syllabus.

I sat in the right corner of class and began my college career. Little did I know that the girl sitting in the front left corner of the class would be the person I spend the next 30 years with. College has a way, college has a way. As the year began, I was struggling to make the transition from high school dropout/janitor to college freshman.

Still dealing with the childhood trauma of watching my father pass in front of me just ten years ago. I leaned heavily on my mom's brother Uncle Duddy. Uncle Duddy told the brutal truth, just like my mother. With that being said there was nowhere to run when you wanted to practice cognitive dissidence. Uncle Duddy blatantly informed me that if I did go to school, be prepared to overcome adversity.

I would be wasting my time and might as well come over to the community college and pick up a trade if I don't keep focused. I informed him that I will make him proud. It wasn't long before I realized that I had not properly prepared myself to succeed in college, so I immediately learned that sacrifice and perseverance is the required cost for lack of preparation. I began by adding a class each semester to my schedule until I was prepared to be a full-time student financially and otherwise.

8 CAPTIAN IN MY SOUL

Focused, determined and driven by the fear of failure. I trusted time and patience, understanding they were my only allies. After three semesters, I became a full-time student. I began adjusting and organizing my life to my mission. I needed to adjust.

The first obstacles were going to class and ignoring the baby freaknic that existed at the forty-five-minute mark of every hour. Fighting the urge to go to the student parking lot and hoping in my rimmed out, dropped Mazda RX-7, cruising the campus a few rounds looking for females matching the same energy. My adjustment was a simple one, sacrifice and focus.

Barely knowing how to add fractions. I scheduled my classes with an hour between each. Once class ended I proceeded to the top floor of the John B. Cade Library. Entering through the doubled doors into a beige colored lobby and on to the elevators which carried me to the fourth floor to review and work on whatever was covered in the previous class.

I began seeing the bigger picture. As I silently walked down the sloped pathway over the Mississippi basin, passing by the Scott's Bluff version of a rainforest. I listened to the synchronized chirping of mole crickets, carried by the live oak trees and rhythmic chirping of blue jays with a Louisiana Mockingbird keeping everything in rhythm. This walk I would also make hundreds of times over the next few years. Slowly approaching what was referred to as the back of the campus.

I noticed a few cows grazing and the smell of chickens in the Southern University poultry facility. I entered a small white building 25 years past due on a coat of paint. To begin what would be a very enlightening 3 ½ years as an Animal Science Major. During the next 3 ½ years it was all about the grind. Working, studying, a fiancé', apartment living and attempting to play football. The struggle was real. There were many successes and many failures.

> **Our greatest glory is not in never falling, but in rising every time we fall.**
>
> — Confucius

As I sat alongside the steamy Lakes of Louisiana State University, my place of refuge, my Zen. I watched the burnt orange glow of sunlight create a calming backdrop to Death Valley. A sense of understanding and peace overcame my spirit as I watched the dance of wildlife, insects and humidity, creating a quietude and calmness that only the Lakes could provide. During these times I thought strongly about my failures. I had very few successes.

I understood that in order to be successful I must have the enthusiasm to embrace failure. Accepting the spiritual growth that comes from knowing that I gave something my all and there is more that I must give to reach my highest potential. I understood that to achieve greatness, I must be great now. I asked myself, what is great now? It means, to never give up, never turn off the light switch of success.

It means to set expectations of myself in all that I do and hold myself accountable to those expectations with every breath in my body. If done correctly and consistently. Time becomes only a measuring tool used to monitor events of growth. It is no longer an assessment of success. From that moment I became my future. Proudly existing in my present.

I can remember awaking to the sound of south Louisiana bird migration. The smell of clovers and morning dew on St. Augustine grass was seeping through the rectangular window pane above my head. For a brief moment, lost in the beauty of a Louisiana morning I forgot what day it was. It was my first day at work and I had every reason to be excited, nervous and totally enthused.

Knowing that today would be just a regular but not so regular day for me of course. As reality set in, I realized that I was about to attend my first faculty meeting at my old high school. Eight years prior, I failed to graduate with my class, dropped out and received my diploma six years after walking through its doors for the first time as a freshman. Would My former teachers see me as the man I had become?

College graduate with a Bachelor's degree in Animal Science Pre - Veterinary Medicine, husband, father, coach. Somewhat ashamed, yet extremely proud of my journey, and my process. I plowed through those waves and went to work. As I walked, from the bedroom into the main room of our home. My wife, also dressed for work, was cooking the usual bacon, eggs and toast sandwich. My son played on the floor as my black lab Ebony observed him attempting to master his first steps. I could smell the aroma of butter and bacon as I had my whole life. She quietly asked "are you ready?" I paused, and said "Hell yeah."

Made in the USA
Middletown, DE
04 April 2023